CHINA

CHINA
THE LAND AND ITS PEOPLE

EARLY
PHOTOGRAPHS
BY
JOHN THOMSON

約翰温訥出版社
JOHN WARNER PUBLICATIONS
香港 HONG KONG

First published 1873 as
Illustrations Of China And Its People
by Sampson Low, Marston, Low and Searle, London

Revised and edited 1977 by John Warner
Second edition 1979

Published by John Warner Publications
P.O.Box 6751, General Post Office, Hong Kong

Filmset by T.P. Graphic Arts Services, Hong Kong
Printed in Hong Kong by the Government Printer

International Standard Book Number 962 7015 02 4

CONTENTS

FOREWORD

John Thomson was born in Edinburgh in 1837. Few details of his early life are known but before he left Scotland for his first visit to the Far East in 1860, he had gained a reputation as an architectural photographer.

It would be inevitable that a young man living in Edinburgh and interested in photography should come under the influence of the city's pioneer photographers, who included David Octavius Hill and Robert Adamson. Although their remarkable work was compressed into a short period of only four years (before Thomson could have been seriously interested in photography), they improved on Henry Fox Talbot's calotype process by effectively reducing exposure times. In addition they had the inspiration to take the camera out of the confines of the studio into the outside world. To many in and around Edinburgh, Hill and Adamson taught not only technique but also conveyed the message that now it was possible for the first time to spontaneously portray people of all walks of life in natural surroundings.

The invention of the wet collodion process by Frederick Scott Archer in London in 1850 further dramatically reduced the all important exposure time. It was this process which was adopted by John Thomson in the course of his travels.

Quite what possessed John Thomson at the age of twenty-four to depart by P & O steamer to the Far East is a matter for speculation. He was certainly more than a gifted photographer with an advanced technique on the look-out for unusual subjects. To set off at all on such a journey required a spirit of adventure and the curiosity of an explorer. To record his travels and observations, as he was later to do, also required an education, the will to research and the ability to write. Unfortunately the first journey proved a short one and after visiting Singapore and Cambodia he returned home a sick man.

His second journey was longer and more ambitious. Details of his actual movements are scanty but he seems to have arrived back in Malaya in early 1864. He spent ten months in Penang and Wellesley Province before setting up a photographic studio in Singapore in 1865. Later that year he visited Siam and in the following year Cambodia and Indo-China.

Thomson probably arrived in Hong Kong in 1868. Here he began his study of China and his photography of this land and its people.

Photographers familiar with the use of today's miniature camera will find it hard to imagine the hardships and herculean labours which faced the travelling photographer using the wet collodion process, more than a century ago.

With photographic enlargements unknown, large pictures required large wooden box-type cameras capable of accommodating glass plates of 10×12 inches and 12×16 inches (even a giant 22×28 inches was not unknown). Several lenses and a sturdy tripod would also be required. For the coating and sensitizing of the plates and the developing and fixing of the image, a complete chest of chemicals was needed. This processing had to be carried out immediately before and after exposure of the plate in total darkness. A portable light-proof tent big enough to house the entire dark room outfit—dishes, glass measures, funnels, scales, weights, etc., as well as the photographer, was essential, as was a bucket and a supply of fresh water. With this equipment and these supplies, Thomson sought to penetrate a largely unknown and unapproachable China, "with the aid of eight to ten bearers." In his Introduction and at times in his narrative, he relates some of the difficulties which he encountered in the five or so years he spent in China.

John Thomson left China in 1872 and returned to London to live in Brixton in the south of the city. Here he spent a good deal of his time writing not only about his travels, but also translating and editing Gaston Tissandier's 'History and Handbook of Photography'.

The following year he produced his remarkable photographs of street life in London, and in 1878 he was off on his travels once more to photograph the latest addition to the British Empire—Cyprus.

After this last journey overseas, Thomson established a fashionable studio at 70a, Grosvenor Street, London and became a pioneer in the field of 'at home' portraits of famous people. His interest in travel was maintained through the Royal Geographical Society of which Thomson was a Fellow. He offered his services as photographic instructor to its members before they set out on their expeditions.

His own work in China seems to have retained a special life-long interest for Thomson. He wrote four books on the subject, the last one, 'Through China with a Camera' published in 1898, twenty-five years after his travels. All except 'Illustrations of China and Its People' which, when it appeared in 1873 cost over £12, contain engravings made from Thomson's photographs, in the interests of economy. The two hundred photographs in 'Illustrations of China and Its People' were printed by the newly invented collotype process and fortunately the quality has made it possible to reproduce direct from this book (with a few exceptions).

Time and changed attitudes have made some of these photographs un-interesting and these have been excluded, while a small number of unpublished photographs have been added. Thomson's text, which frequently displays remarkable knowledge, insight and wit, has been edited without drastically changing its commendable style, to provide manageable captions to the photographs. The section which was originally devoted to Taiwan has been omitted as this was concerned exclusively with a tribal minority incidental to the main them of the work—mainland China.

'Illustrations of China and Its People' is now generally recognised as being a unique work of photo-journalism. It was the first photographic social documentation of any kind to be published, predating Thomson's own 'Street Life in London' by four years. John Thomson is also regarded as the most eminent photographer to have visited China in the nineteenth century.

In the course of his journey of nearly 5,000 miles, he combines his remarkable talents as a portraitist and landscapist. He shows an equal curiosity as an observer of strange monuments and an unfamiliar landscape as he does for the customs, occupations and appearance of the Chinese people. He is faced with a country of contradictions and injustices most of all between the rich and the poor, the powerful and the humble. Nowhere is this contrast more evident than between his formal portraits of the rulers and gentry and his eloquent studies of anonymous people in the streets. Here we sense a corrupt and remote government, the poverty of the land and the backwardness and ignorance of the people. There is no mistaking that Thomson's sympathies lie with the humble and deprived. His unfashionable photographs of artisans, beggars and labourers are deeply moving and aesthetic images.

Thomson's *'Illustrations of China and Its People'* is a portrayal of a fragile nation where change seems inevitable and revolution a distinct possibility. This prophetic quality gives a sense of actuality to his work. These remarkable photographs remain as vivid today as they were a hundred years ago.

Hong Kong 1977   JOHN WARNER

John Thomson. Detail from a group photograph

8

INTRODUCTION

My design is to present a series of pictures of China and its people, such as shall convey an accurate impression of the country as well as of the arts, usages, and manners which prevail in different provinces of the Empire. With this intention I made the camera the constant companion of my wanderings, and to it I am indebted for the faithful reproduction of the scenes I visited, and of the people with whom I came into contact.

Those familiar with the Chinese and their deeply-rooted superstitions will readily understand that the carrying out of my task involved both difficulty and danger. In some places there were many who had never yet set eyes upon a pale-faced stranger; and the literati, or educated classes, had fostered a notion amongst such as these, that, while evil spirits of every kind were carefully to be shunned, none ought to be so strictly avoided as the "Fan Qui" or "Foreign Devil," who assumed human shape, and appeared solely for the furtherance of his own interests, often owing the success of his undertakings to an ocular power, which enabled him to discover the hidden treasures of heaven and earth. I therefore frequently enjoyed the reputation of being a dangerous geomancer, and my camera was held to be a dark mysterious instrument which, combined with my naturally, or supernaturally, intensified eyesight gave me power to see through rocks and mountains, to pierce the very souls of the people and to produce miraculous pictures by some black art, which at the same time bereft the individual depicted of so much of the principle of life as to render his death a certainty within a very short period of years.

Accounted, for these reasons, the forerunner of death, I found portraits of children difficult to obtain, while, strange as it may be thought in a land where filial piety is esteemed the highest of virtues, sons and daughters brought their aged parents to be placed before the foreigner's silent and mysterious instrument of destruction. The trifling sums that I paid for the privilege of taking such subjects would probably go to help in the purchase of a coffin, which, conveyed ceremoniously to the old man's house, would there be deposited to await the hour of dissolution, and the body of the parent whom his son had honoured with the gift. Let none of my readers suppose that I am speaking in jest. To such an extreme pitch has the notion of honouring ancestors with due mortuary rites been carried in China, that an affectionate parent would regard children who should present him with a cool and comfortable coffin as having begun in good time to display the duty and respect which every well-regulated son and daughter is expected to bestow.

The superstitious influences, such as I have described, rendered me a frequent object of mistrust, and led to my being stoned and roughly handled on more occasions than one. It is, however, in and about large cities that the wide-spread hatred of foreigners is most conspicuously displayed. In many of

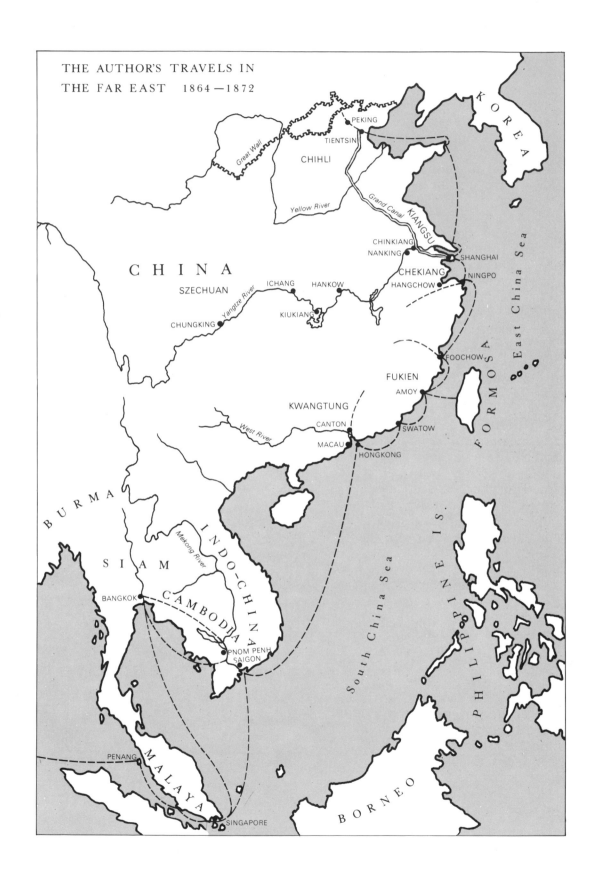

THE AUTHOR'S TRAVELS IN
THE FAR EAST 1864—1872

KOREA

Great Wall

PEKING

TIENTSIN

CHIHLI

Yellow River

Grand Canal

KIANGSU

East China Sea

C H I N A

CHINKIANG

NANKING

SHANGHAI

CHEKIANG

NINGPO

SZECHUAN

Yangtze River

ICHANG

HANKOW

HANGCHOW

CHUNGKING

KIUKIANG

FOOCHOW

FORMOSA

FUKIEN

AMOY

KWANGTUNG

West River

CANTON

SWATOW

MACAU

HONGKONG

BURMA

INDO-CHINA

Mekong River

SIAM

CAMBODIA

BANGKOK

PHILIPPINE IS.

PNOM PENH
SAIGON

South China Sea

PENANG

MALAYA

BORNEO

SINGAPORE

the country districts, and from officials who have been associated with Europeans, I have met with numerous tokens of kindness, and a hospitality as genuine as could be shown to a stranger in any part of the world.

It is a novel experiment to attempt to illustrate a book of travels with photographs, a few years back so perishable, and so difficult to reproduce. I feel somewhat sanguine about the success of the undertaking, and I hope to see the process which I have thus applied adopted by other travellers; for the faithfulness of such pictures affords the nearest approach that can be made towards placing the reader actually before the scene which is represented.

The text which accompanies the pictures, and which will render them, as I trust, more interesting and more intelligible, is compiled from information derived from the most trustworthy sources, as well as from notes either made by me at the time the subjects were taken, or gathered during a residence of nearly five years in China.

I have endeavoured to arrange these notes and illustrations as far as possible in the natural order or sequence of my journeys, which extended over a distance, estimated roughly, of between 4,000 and 5,000 miles.

I shall start from the British colony of Hong Kong, once said to be the grave of Europeans, but which now, with its city of Victoria, its splendid public buildings, parks and gardens, its docks, factories, telegraphs and fleets of steamers, may be fairly considered the birthplace of a new era in eastern civilization. I will next proceed by the Pearl river to Canton, the city above all others possessing the greatest historical interest to foreigners, as the scene of their early efforts to gain a footing in the country. Thence I will cross to Formosa, an island which, by its tropical luxuriance and by the grandeur of its mountain scenery, deserves the name 'Isla Formosa' which the early Portuguese voyagers conferred upon it. Returning to the mainland, I will visit Swatow and Chaochow, noted for the quality of their sugar and rice, for their turbulent clans, and for village wars that remind one of the feudal times of Scotland.

I shall then pass northward to Amoy, remarkable in modern times as that part of the Fukien province from which a constant tide of emigration flows to the Straits of Malacca and to America, and noticeable also for the independent character of its people, as among the last who succumbed to the Tartar yoke.

Following the route northward the reader will next be introduced to Shanghai, the greatest of the treaty ports of China, where, within a few years, a foreign settlement has sprung up, on the banks of the Woosung, of such vast proportions, as to lead a visitor to fancy that he has been suddenly transported to one of our great English ports. Leaving Shanghai, I will proceed to Ningpo and Snowy Valley, the favourite spring resort of Shanghai residents, and justly celebrated for the beauty of its azaleas, its mountain scenery, its cascades and waterfalls; thence to the Yangtsze Kiang, visiting *en route* the treaty ports and the ancient capital, Nankin, passing through the weird scenery of the gorges of the Upper Yangtsze, and penetrating as far as Kweichow. The concluding journey will embrace Chefoo, the Peiho, Tientsin and Peking. The remarkable antiquities, the palace, temples, and observatory; the different races in the great metropolis; the ruins of the Summer Palace and the Ming Tombs shall be presented to the reader: after which I will guide him through the Nankow Pass, and take my leave of him at the Great Wall.

London 1873   JOHN THOMSON

I
KWANGTUNG
HONGKONG MACAU CANTON

2

1   Pagoda in Canton (*title page*)
2   A Canton Junk Near Amoy

3   A Young Cantonese Boat Girl
4   On Board A Junk

The term junk, applied by Europeans to all Chinese craft, whether trading vessels or ships of war, is probably derived from 'djong', the Javanese word for a large boat or vessel. Chinese ships vary in dimensions, model and appearance, in the different parts of the Empire as much as do the sailing craft of Europe. This vessel under sail (No 2) is a coasting trader of Kwangtung build, and may be regarded as one of the clipper fleet of southern China. It looks heavy and unhandy, but it will make good sailing in a fair wind. The great eyes and the configuration about the stem resembling the head and features of a fierce sea-monster, are intended to scare away the deep sea-demons that might at any time impede the voyage. The mat sails, with their ribs of bamboo, still look like the spread wings of a huge bat, or the fiery dragon of the Celestial mythology.

These vessels are frequently owned and sailed by a party of small traders, a number of the better class of sailors having a venture in the cargo as well. This complication of petty interests and the absence of a recognized commander, or indeed anyone scientifically trained in navigation, leads to constant disputes. In a case of emergency such as a storm, a consultation takes place as to the fittest mode of handling the vessel, and the decision is frequently referred for final settlement to 'Machu' the sailor's goddess, who has a shrine set apart for her on board.

It is customary before proceeding on a voyage to offer sacrifice to 'Machu'. A cock is decapitated and its blood, together with some of its feathers, are stuck to the bow and foremast, a small cup of wine is at the same time cast over the bow into the sea.

Sailing, as I have above observed, is managed, not by the study of the compass, barometer, or by astronomical observations, but by a knowledge of the currents and headlands and the prevailing winds of the season. The compass is used, but it is an instrument of primitive construction, having a very small tremulous needle in the centre of a disc of wood, covered with a formidable array of Chinese symbols, astrological and others. It seems strange that the reputed inventors of the mariner's compass should have left to other nations the merit of applying it to its proper scientific use.

3

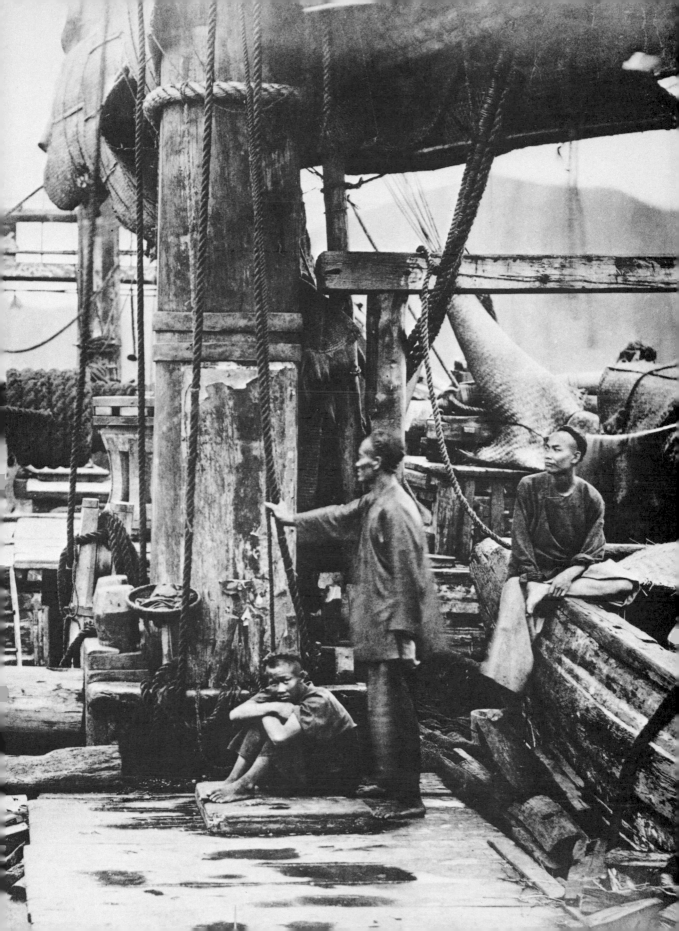

5

5, 6 Canton Boat People

Many thousands of the population of Canton pass their lives in their boats. These floating dwellings afford many advantages to their poor owners who, had they to live on land, would be crowded into miserable makeshift hovels in the unhealthiest quarters of the city. There they would have to inhale the polluted air of a neglected neighbourhood, as even in the most fashionable localities of a Chinese city all sanitary regulations are ignored. In a boat the owner finds profitable employment for himself and his family, and can shift his anchorage at pleasure.

The old woman in the photograph is the grandmother who still works cheerfully at the oar, and nurses, all the while, one of the grandchildren.

The girls are two daughters of a respectable boating family. They have been trained in the use of the oar and the management of boats, from earliest childhood. Hundreds of the small passenger boats that ply for hire about the wharves of Canton, are managed by young girls, whose pride it is to keep them bright and attractive-looking.

7　Hong Kong

This photograph is taken from the residence of Mr. Jardine at East Point. On the left is the entrance to Wong Nei Chong or Happy Valley, noted for its picturesque hill scenery, its racecourse and its cemetery for Europeans. The eminence to the left is Morrison's Hill, crowned with a row of substantially built foreign residences. In the foreground are to be seen the opium godowns of Messrs Jardine Matheson.

8　Smoking Opium

Opium-smoking is one of the most enslaving vices which, when it has secured its victim, gradually poisons and destroys the finer feelings of his nature, causing him to neglect his business, dispose of his property, and even sever the sacred ties of kindred by selling his wife and children into slavery so that he may gratify his ruling passion. When once indulged in, it is difficult and sometimes dangerous, to throw off

the habit.

The drug sold in the low public opium-shops is of inferior quality, being mixed with opium ash in its preparation. These shops or dens have a noxious atmosphere, heavy with the fumes of opium which, added to the livid and death-like appearance of the smokers stretched upon the benches, recalls the horrors of a nightmare.

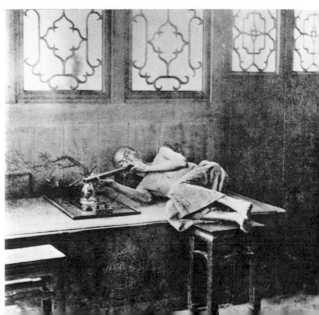

9   The Praya, Hong Kong

The Praya (for so the Portuguese term the broad stone-faced road along the harbour in front of the city) affords a pleasant drive some miles in extent, and joins the route to Shau Kei Wan in Lei Yue Mun Pass through which we approach the port from the east. This view is taken from the front of the Parade ground and represents the principal business part of the Praya. The block of buildings facing the water on the left are the premises of the Hong Kong and Shanghai and Chartered Mercantile Banks. The huge edifice in the centre was erected by Messrs Dent. The merchants commonly have their offices on the ground floor and reside in the chambers above; there they command an extensive view of the harbour as they promenade in spacious verandahs 'when the wind bloweth in from the sea.'

I must not omit to mention the flagstaff shown on the Peak above the city: one of the early institutions of the Colony and to which a resident signalman and code of signals are attached. Few who have made Hong Kong for any time their home, have not watched with earnestness the bare post and spars of the signal staff and experienced a sense of relief, or a quickened pulsation, as they noticed the little flag unfurled, and the flash from the Peak gun, that heralded the arrival of the mail in the harbour.

9

10

10   Hong Kong Harbour

In this view, taken when the Duke of Edinburgh visited Hong Kong in 1869, HMS 'Galatea' is seen at anchor off Peddar's Wharf. Those familiar with the place will readily recognize the well-known range of hills that shelters the harbour on the Kowloon side.

11　The Clock Tower, Hong Kong

The Clock Tower designed by Mr. Rawlings in 1861, is a great ornament to the city, the clock too, when regulated properly, is of no inconsiderable service. It has however, been a victim to the climate, and is liable to fits of indisposition, resting from its duties at the most inconvenient seasons, as if unable to contend against the heat. The tower is seen to advantage from the harbour, and the lighted dial of the clock forms a good landmark to guide the benighted steersman to the landing steps of Peddar's Wharf. In this street stand several of the oldest buildings in the Colony. On the right of this picture we see the residence lately occupied by Messrs Hunt and Co; and on the left is shown a part of the west wing of the palatial building erected by Messrs Dent, when commerce was most flourishing in the settlement. Also on the left and nearest the tower, stands the Hong Kong Hotel, constructed after the model of the larger hotels in London.

13   After Dinner

This is an after dinner gathering on the verandah of a Chinese home. The entire domestic circle smoke tobacco. The old woman and her daughter use a pipe which resembles the 'hookah'. Paterfamilias is fondling and sucking the end of what appears to be a formidable walking stick, but is in reality his favourite pipe. There is among the Chinese the same after-dinner companionship in smoking which in our own country strengthens the social ties; but with this important difference, that in China the ladies smoke.

12   The Toilet

The ladies of China are skilled in the use of cosmetics; but their ways are not as our ways. No well regulated Chinese beauty would be guilty of washing her face; it must be polished with a hot damp cloth. When this process is over, the surface is ready to receive its coating of finely prepared white powder, after which the smooth whitened skin is tinted with carmine. The powder, carmine, comb, hairbrush, tooth-brush, tongue scraper, gum, hairpins and all the other appliances of the feminine toilet are pre-served in a small brass or silver bound dressing case carrying a mirror within the lid.

Lamqua was a Chinese pupil of Chinnery, a noted foreign artist, who died at Macau in 1852. Lamqua produced a number of excellent works in oil which are still copied by the painters in Hong Kong and Canton. Had he lived in any other country he would have been the founder of a school of painting. In China his followers have failed to grasp the spirit of his art. They drudge with imitative servile toil, copying Lamqua's or Chinnery's pieces, or anything, no matter what, and at so much a square foot. There are a number of painters established in Hong Kong, but they all do the same class of work which consists mainly in making enlarged copies of photographs.

    The best works these painters do are pictures of native and foreign ships, which are wonderfully drawn.

14

14   A Musician

16   A Mendicant Priest

This priest is attached to the Kwan Yin Temple. His duty is to beg for the benefit of the establishment and to perform unimportant offices for the visitors to the shrine, lighting incense sticks and teaching short forms of prayer. He is a type of the thousands of miserable, half-starved hangers-on of monastic establishments to be found in China.

17   Kwan Yin Temple

This is a small temple on the hillside to the east of the city. It is dedicated to Kwan Yin, Goddess of Mercy, and is liberally supported by the Chinese of Hong Kong. Like the majority of Chinese temples, it has been erected in a position naturally picturesque, surrounded by fine old trees and shady walks, commanding an extensive view of the harbour. A never-ceasing crowd of beggars infest the broad granite steps by which the temple is approached, and prey upon the charitably disposed who make visits to the shrine.

The rule in China, from earliest times, has been to confer rank and honours of the highest grade only on men distinguished for rare genius or exceptional literary attainments. By the system of periodical literary examinations established in the chief cities of the Empire, even the poorest student may win his way to a proud position in the government of his country. Of course, in so large a community many unsuccessful candidates for literary distinction are to be found. Such a one is the venerable scholar in the photograph. He is convinced that there must have been some mistake, or some underhand influences operating in the examinations to which he has been subjected from time to time.

18

18　A School Boy

I have heard the industry and aptitude of the Chinese school boy highly praised by those who have had experience in teaching European and Chinese children side by side; and I am assured that, notwithstanding the obvious disadvantages under which the latter labour in having to acquire a foreign language and foreign habits of thought, their capacity for learning is so great that it will sustain them neck and neck in the race with their European rivals.

20   Macau

The principal residences front the bay, round
which runs a broad carriage-drive, known as
the Praya Grande, shown in the illustration. This
picture was taken from the hill above Bishop's

Bay at the southern extremity of the Praya. The inner harbour is on the north-west side of the peninsula where the oldest part of the town is to be found.

21   Jui Lin, Viceroy Of The Two Kwang Provinces

The Viceroy of Kwangtung and Kwangsi is one of the highest dignitaries in the Chinese Empire and at the same time is, perhaps, of all Chinese officials the most widely known by Europeans. A Manchu by birth, Jui Lin became at an early age employed in public functions at the capital and, having gained the favour of the Emperor Tao-kuang, he rose to high employ, reaching the rank of cabinet minister when about forty-five years of age.

In 1864 he was appointed to fill the important office of general commanding the Tartar garrison of Canton. In the following year he became Viceroy of the two provinces. The importance of his position, and the proximity of Hong Kong to his seat of government, combined to bring him into frequent personal relations with European officials, with whom his intercourse has invariably been marked by perfect courtesy and an obvious desire to cultivate friendly relations.

22   Looking North From The Po Lo Hang
      Temple, Kwangtung

23   Tartar Soldiers, Canton

The Manchus, commonly called Tartars, conquered China in 1644, but it was not until 24th November 1650 that Canton was taken. After the overthrow of Canton, the Tartars following the plan which they had adopted in Peking and other cities of the Empire, established a permanent garrison of Tartars and of the Chinese and Mongols who had sided with them. They were divided under eight banners distinguished by colours, red, blue, yellow, etc. Their encampment remains to this day, occupying about one-fourth of the entire area of the city.

The bannermen of Canton number 1,800 many of them being extremely poor; for although their nominal pay is good it never reaches the recipient in full. The government pittance is thus insufficient to support them, and, while during the past two centuries they have been steadily losing their national characteristics, they have scorned to imitate the patient industry of the Chinese, or adopt their trades and occupations. Thoroughly drilled and disciplined they would still make good soldiers.

The reader cannot fail to be struck with the fine manly build and soldierly appearance of the Tartar artillerymen shown in the photograph. These men formed the guard of Sir D.B. Robertson, our consul at Canton.

23

24 Physic Street, Canton

The streets of a Chinese city differ greatly from those of Europe, and are always extremely narrow, except in Nanking and Peking. They are paved with stone slabs, usually worn down by the traffic to a hollow in the centre of the path, by which means the rain water is carried off. The shops are nearly all uniform in size; all have one apartment which opens upon the street, and a granite or brick counter for the purpose of displaying their wares. A granite base also supports the upright signboard which is the indispensable characteristic of every shop in China.

Opposite the signboard stands a small altar or shrine dedicated to the God who presides over the tradesman and his craft. This deity is honoured regularly when the shop is opened, and a small incense stick is lit and kept burning in a bronze cup of ashes placed in front of the shrine.

The shops within are frequently fitted with a counter of polished wood and finely carved shelves, while at the back is an accountant's room, screened off with an openwork wooden partition carved to resemble a climbing plant.

Physic Street, or more correctly, Hsiang Lan Street, is one of the finest in Canton and, with its varied array of brightly coloured signboards, presents an appearance no less interesting than picturesque.

The signboards may be taken as fair examples of the street literature of China, showing the national tendency of the shop-keepers to introduce their commonest wares by some high-flown classical phrase having, as far as I can see, no reference whatever to the contents of the shop. Tien I (Celestial advantage) for example, offers a thoroughly terrestrial advantage to customers in the shape of covers and cushions; and why, one might be tempted to ask, should swallows' nests be a 'Sign of the Eternal?'

These phrases are however, simply intended as the signs or names by which each shop is known:-

Chien Chi Hao, the sign of the symbol Chien (Heaven). Hweichow ink, pencils and writing requisites.

Chang Chi T'ang (Chang of the family branch designated Chi). Wax-cased pills of select manufacture.

Tien I (Celestial advantage). Table-covers, chair-covers, cushions and rattan mats.

Tien I Shen (Celestial advantage combined with attention).

Yung Chi (Sign of the Eternal). Swallows' nests.

Money-schroffing taught here.

Ai Wen T'ang. The Hall of delight in scholarship. Seals artistically carved.

26   Schroffing Dollars

Schroffing or testing and examining dollars is an operation conducted by the comprador's staff to ascertain that no counterfeit coin has been introduced. In transferring the dollars from one sack to another, two are taken up at a time, poised upon the tips of the fingers, struck and sounded, the tone of base metal being readily detected. The milling of the edge is also examined, as the Chinese show great cleverness in sawing the dollar asunder, scraping out and reuniting the two halves, which they fill up with a hard solder made of a cheap metal that when rung emits a clear silver tone. So deftly is the reuniting done, that none but an expert can detect the junction of the two halves.

25   A Comprador

This comprador or treasurer in a foreign mercantile house, by his legitimate savings and private trading speculations, has accumulated a large fortune. It is the common practice of foreign merchants to employ a Chinese of known repute and ability to act as treasurer to the firm. He is a leading man among the local merchants and one whose intimate knowledge of foreign business diffuses a widespread influence among the wealthy traders. The comprador is the head of his clan. All the staff are engaged by him and he it is who is held responsible for their honesty and good behaviour.

25

26

45

27,28   The Bride and Bridegroom

It is customary for the poorer members of society
to hire their bridal dresses from a costumier.
The prevailing colour of the bride's dress is red.

    The bridgroom is at liberty to wear the robes
of a mandarin, thus showing the high esteem
in which the relationship of marriage is held by
the State. He too wears red in the form of a
bridal scarf thrown over the shoulder.

29   A Canton Lady

A lady in China passes her life in strict seclusion. Her little world is her home, her companions the ladies of her own household or relatives of her own sex. If she pays a visit, a sedan chair conveys her from her own door; silken curtains screen her from the public gaze; and thus protected she is borne to the ladies' quarter in her friend's home, with privacy and concealment.

30   The Lady's Maid

This maid is a slave-girl, bought in childhood for a trifling sum from poor parents. This girl has been reared in the bosom of the family and trained to wait on the ladies, to attend to the children and to make herself generally useful. In this picture she is represented on her way to market, the slave enjoying more freedom in going abroad than does her mistress.

31 Tea Picking In Canton

In former times, before Hankow or the Yangtsze River was thrown open to foreign trade, all the tea from the great Tung Ting Lake district was brought to Canton for exportation. The bulk of the tea shipped nowadays from Canton is grown in Kwangtung, of which province that city is the capital.

From the leaf of the Tai Shan plantations, which are the most noted in that neighbourhood, the 'Canton District Congou' and the 'Long Leaf Scented Orange Pekoe' are manufactured. These teas are prepared by twisting the leaf in the hand; when so twisted it frequently shows a small white feathery tip at the end of the leaf, known as the 'Pekoe tip'.

Lo Ting leaf makes 'Scented Caper' and Gunpowder teas. These teas are rolled in a bag with the feet until the leaf is twisted into round pellets.

Macao is the port from which the bulk of District Congous are exported and Canton is famous for its Scented Capers and Scented Orange Pekoe. The green tea trade from Canton is of secondary importance, this tea being chiefly exported to the continental countries of Europe.

The cultivation of tea in Kwangtung is on the increase and the preparation of tea for the foreign markets is carried on extensively at Canton. The Congou and Pekoe teas are brought down from the plantations, rolled by hand, dried in the sun, and then they are in a condition suitable for subsequent firing and preparation for the market.

Black teas, after being partially dried in the sun, and slightly fired, are rolled either by the palm of the hand on a flat tray, or by foot in a hempen bag. They are scorched in iron pans over a slow charcoal fire, and after this spread out on bamboo trays, that the broken stems and refuse leaves may be picked out. It is this operation, which is performed by women and children, that is shown in the photograph. The teas are then separated by passing them through sieves, so as to form different sizes and qualities of tea.

32   Rolling Scented Caper And Gunpowder Teas

The manipulation required to produce Gunpowder tea is one of the most curious and interesting of all the processes to which the leaf is submitted. Coolies, resting their arms on a cross-beam, with their feet busily roll and toss balls, of perhaps a foot in diameter, up and down the floor. The balls consist of canvas bags packed full of tea leaves, which by the constant rolling motion assume the pellet shape. The scent or bouquet of the tea is imparted after the final drying or scorching, by the addition of flower petals, which are removed by sieving before packing.

33   Weighing The Tea For Export

Lead-lined chests, soldered up and ready for exportation are piled in symmetrical blocks in the weighing room of the Chinese tea-house. The inspector places his mark upon a score or more of chests and asks for them to be removed, opened and examined. This done they are conveyed to the scales and weighed.

32

33

51

35 A Tea-Tasting Room, Canton

Two Chinese tea merchants in a foreign taster's room, await an offer for their samples. Every foreign house in Canton that does any trade in tea has a room specially fitted up for the accommodation of the taster. The windows of the room face north and are screened off so as to admit a steady light which falls directly on the tea-board. Upon this board the samples are spread in square wooden trays and it is under the uniform light that the minute inspection of colour, make and appearance of the leaves take place. On the shelves around the room stand rows of tin boxes, identical in size and shape, containing registered samples of the teas of former years. These are used for reference. Even the cups, uniform in design and regularly arranged in rows along the tables, have been manufactured especially for the business of tasting tea.

The samples are placed in these cups and hot water of a given temperature is then poured upon them. The time the tea rests in the cups is measured by a sand-glass and when this is done all is ready for tasting. All the tests are made by assistants who have gone through a special course of training which fits them for the mysteries of their art.

34

34 A Cantonese Pawnshop

The square tower in the photograph is a specimen of the pawnshops throughout the south of China. Within, on the ground floor, is the office for the transaction of business, and thence a square wooden scaffolding standing free of the inner walls, runs right up to the roof. This scaffolding is divided into a series of floors, having ladders as their main approach. On the ground floor are stowed pledges of the greatest bulk, such as furniture. The smaller and lighter articles occupy the upper floors, while the one nearest the roof is exclusively for jewellery or other property of great intrinsic value. Every pledge from floor to ceiling is catalogued, and carries a ticket denoting the number of the article and the date on which it was deposited. An iron railing and a narrow footpath run round the outside of the roof, and a store of heavy stones is piled up there, to be hurled upon the head of a robber, should he attempt to scale the wall.

35

36 The Temple Of The Five Hundred Gods

This celebrated shrine, which the Chinese call 'Magnificent Forest Temple', is situated in the western suburbs of Canton. The Hall of Saints, shown in this photograph, forms the chief attraction of the place. This Hall contains five hundred gilded effigies of saints out of the Buddhist calendar.

37 The Abbot

The Chief Priest of this Temple, who had spent half his lifetime in this secluded place, was greatly devoted to his flowers. Among them was a splendid specimen of the sacred lotus in full bloom. He received us with great courtesy and hospitality, which I enjoyed in all the Buddhist establishments I visited throughout my travels in China.

36

37

38   Pun Shi Cheng's Garden, Canton

39   Honan Temple

Honan Temple, one of the largest Buddhist establishments in the south of China, stands on the southern bank of the Pearl River at Canton.

40   The Old Factory Site, Canton

In 1684 a small patch of land on the bank of the
river at Canton was granted to the East India
Company with permission to erect a factory
there, provided all their traders and trading
operations were strictly confined within its circuit. This site, with its present boundary wall
and buildings, is shown in the photograph, and
now forms the American Concession Ground,
its buildings being occupied by Messrs Russell
and Messrs Smith and Archer, two of the oldest
American houses in China.

41   Military Official
42   The Sedan
43   A Public Sedan

The sedan chair is one of the most useful institutions in China and has been employed there from a very ancient date. Private sedans are kept by civil mandarins and by people of wealth and rank. In former days strict rules existed which forbade certain of the lower orders and even foreigners, from using sedans. With the civil mandarins the sedan is the official means of conveyance, their rank being denoted by the covering and furniture of their chairs, as well as by the number of bearers and the footmen in attendance. Military mandarins on the other hand, travel or pay their official visits on horseback.

The chair of the most importance is the Bridal chair. It is richly ornamented and gilded, and is hung with red silk curtains, which screen the blushing fair one on the day of marriage from the intrusive vulgar gaze.

In Hong Kong sedan chairs are the only public conveyances. Chair-stands are to be found in all the hotels, at the corners of the chief thoroughfares, as well as on the wharves, where the eager chair-coolies pounce upon each freshly arrived stranger as he lands at the port. These bearers vie with each other in keeping their chairs clean and attractive-looking, and in displaying to advantage the muscular proportions of their well-formed limbs. During the greater part of the year they have no settled dwelling and sleep in the open air, at some spot where they will wake to find business early astir. They find their food cooked and ready at the street stalls, and they can easily procure substitutes when they wish a few days' leisure and enjoyment.

41

42

43

II
FUKIEN
AMOY FOOCHOW

44 A Pagoda In South China (*title page*)

This picture presents a type of the numberless pagodas which are scattered over the south of China. The one shown here stands on the right bank of the Han river, near Chaochow, and like all the best examples of such edifices, the whole ground structure up to the first storey is composed of stone. Within, a winding staircase gives access to the seven stories of which the tower is made up, and at each storey there is an inner flooring or platform to correspond to the terraces outside. These terraces were originally surrounded by massive stone balustrading, resting on solid ornamental brackets of the same material. The balustrades have in many places been broken away but what still remains is sufficient to show the beauty and the skill with which the stone slabs are dove-tailed into the uprights of the balustrade.

45 Bridge At Chaochow

This bridge over the River Han is perhaps one of the most remarkable in China. Like old London Bridge, with its shops and places of business, the bridge at Chaochow affords space for one of the city markets. It will be seen that the houses are built of light materials, in a very primitive style, and are supported in such a way as to allow a maximum of market space on the causeway; while from a purely sanitary point of view, the houses projecting over the water offer many advantages.

When taking the illustration, I endeavoured to avoid the crowd by starting to work at day-break, but the people were astir, and seeing my strange instrument pointed cannonwise towards their shaky dwellings, they at once decided that I was practising some outlandish witch-craft against the old bridge and its inhabitants. The market stalls were abandoned, that the barbarian who had come to brew mischief for them might be properly pelted. The roughs and market people came heart and soul to the task, armed with mud and missiles, which were soon flying in a shower above my head. I made a plunge for the boat and once on board, it told to my advantage when I charged a ruffian with the pointed tripod as he attempted to stop my progress. My camera lost its cap and received a black eye of mud in exchange. For myself I sustained but little damage, while it may be fairly said that the bridge was taken at the point of the tripod.

46, 47   Foochow Coolies

48–51   Male Heads

Son of a distinguished civil officer of Canton.
He is a fine, attractive little fellow, his full hazel
eyes beaming with kindliness and intelligence.
The face is altogether a pleasing one, but as
is common among children in China, it will
gradually lose its attractions as it grows to
maturity. The softness of the eye is then frequently replaced by a cold, calculating expression, and the countenance assumes an air of
apathetic indifference which is so necessary to
veil the inner feelings of a polished Chinese
gentleman.

   The portrait No 50 will convey an idea of
what this bright little fellow may in time become.
It shows a man whose natural shrewdness
and capacity for business have helped him on
to a successful mercantile career.

   No 49 is the head of a Mongolian, whose
features are heavier than those of the pure
Chinese.

   No 51 is the head of an ordinary Chinese
coolie. He is as a rule, a kindly-disposed person,
quite alive to his own interests, and endowed
by nature with a profound contempt and com-
passion for all barbarians who dwell without
the pale of Chinese civilisation. This will account
for the expression he is casting upon me as I
am about to hand him down to posterity to
be a type for his class.

48

49

50

51

52   Figures In Costume, Amoy
53   The Small Foot Of A Chinese Lady

This picture shows the compressed foot of a
Chinese lady, and I regard it as one of the most
interesting in my collection. I had been assured
that it would be impossible for me, by the offer
of any sum of money, to get a Chinese woman
to unbandage her foot, and yet gold and silver
are arguments in favour of concessions which
operate in the Celestial Empire with more than
usual force. Accordingly, all my efforts failed
until I reached Amoy, and there at last I got
this lady privately conveyed to me in order that
her foot might be photographed. She came
escorted by an old woman whom also I had to
bribe handsomely before she would agree to
countenance an act of such gross indecency as
the unbandaging of the foot of her charge.
And yet, I would rather have avoided the spec-
tacle, for the compressed foot which is figura-
tively supposed to represent a lily, has a very
different appearance and odour from that most
beautiful and sacred of flowers. The process of
compressing the foot begins in early childhood;
the bones of the instep being gradually bent
down by continual bandages till they meet the
heel in such a manner that the smaller toes almost
disappear and become entirely useless. The
cripple is thus reduced to supporting herself
on the great toe and the ball of the heel. The
baneful practice is supposed to have come into
practice about the tenth century. It is argued
it cannot have been of great antiquity because
Confucius and the early writers are silent on
the subject.

52

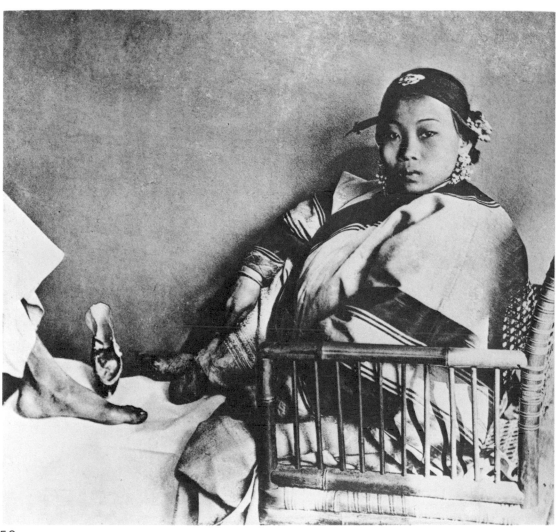

53

54–58 Female Coiffure

A young Cantonese girl of middle class wearing a head-dress which consists of an embroidered belt of satin ornamented with artificial flowers and kingfisher feathers (No 55).

Three Swatow girls (Nos 54, 56, 57) exhibit different styles of coiffure adopted in that province. As will be observed the chignons are each of them different and deserve careful study by ladies of Western lands. The dressing of hair into fantastic forms is naturally a difficult task and one which would shut out spurious imitators in our own country, for few could throw their whole mind and energy into the work. In China with these women, the hair is done once or twice a week. With a view to avoid injuring the elaborate coiffure during sleep, the lady supports the nape of her neck upon a pillar of earthernware or wood, high enough to protect the design from being damaged. In our land this device would imply a sacrifice of comfort, and here and there a case of strangulation would ensue; but no very grave objections could be raised to the novel chignon and its midnight scaffolding, when the interests of fashion are at stake.

No 58 is the chignon par excellence. The lady who wears it is of Ningpo extraction and by profession a barber, who also makes wigs and chignons for sale.

54

55

72

57

56

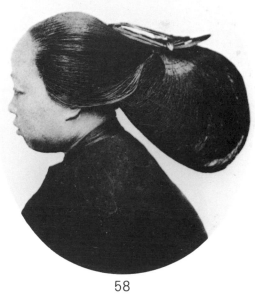

58

59, 60   Actors

The theatre and dramatic performances are highly esteemed in China as a means of entertainment during festive seasons.

It has been incorrectly stated that there are no buildings expressly constructed for theatrical performances to be found in China. There are indeed, none in the majority of Chinese towns; but in Peking and in some other cities which I visited, edifices designed and solely used for dramatic performances do exist. Hong Kong for example, contains two large and imposing theatres devoted exclusively to the representation of Chinese plays.

There are numerous bands of strolling players who may be hired to perform in private dwellings, in temples, or even in sheds erected in the public streets on the occasion of entertainments given by the wealthy to the poor of their neighbourhood.

Chinese actors if popular are well paid. They must however, be men of considerable ability and gifted with retentive memories, for when they are called upon to perform at a feast, it is not unusual for some favoured guest to select a few out of a score or two of plays to be then and there enacted—and many of these actors have to sustain half a dozen different parts. Although well paid they enjoy few privileges, and are not even allowed to compete at literary examinations.

61 The Abbot And Monks Of Kushan Monastery

It is interesting to note how closely the dress of the Buddhist monk resembles the monastic garb of ancient Europe. In both we see a robe, long, simple and ample, falling loosely to the feet; and both carry a cowl for the protection of the head in cold weather, as well as a rosary to aid the wearer in keeping his debtor and creditor account of good and bad thoughts, words and works. This account the Buddhist devotee must privately balance during his hours of meditation, and at the close of every day, until he has reached the supreme degree of sanctity when the principles of good and evil will have ceased to combat in his heart, when the lusts of the flesh will no longer have power to torment, and all the weaknesses of his mortal body are absorbed in that perfect state of comatose ecstasy which is termed in their scriptures 'Nirvana'.

The Buddhists have ten chief commandments which their great teacher left behind for their guidance. These include:
 Thou shalt not kill any living creature
 Thou shalt not steal
 Thou shalt not drink strong liquors
 Thou shalt not eat after the appointed hours
 Thou shalt not have in thy possession either
  a metal figure (an idol) or gold or silver
  or any valuable thing
There are also a multitude of minor laws which have an important place in the regulations of the Buddhist priesthood. Thus at mealtimes:
 Every priest before he eats shall repeat five
  prayers for all the good things which
  have happened to him up to that day
 His heart is to be far from all cupidity and
  lust
 He shall not speak about his dinner, be it
  good or bad
 He shall not smack in eating
 When cleansing his teeth he shall hold
  something before his mouth
These and many more such as these, make up the maxims of Buddha, and except he strictly observes them all, no mortal can attain the bliss of final absorption into 'Nirvana'. If this be indeed true, then the disciples of Sakyamuni in China at the present day have, I fear, but slender prospects of happiness in a future state.

62   Yuen Fu Monastery

This Buddhist monastery is remarkable rather for its romantic situation than for any historical associations. The monastery is about thirty miles distant from Foochow in a very mountainous and richly-wooded country. The sacred edifice rests in a cavern on the summit of a mountain, and is only reached after a tedious and precipitous ascent. Sacred texts from the Classics are everywhere sculptured on the rocks, and it is in a dark recess, resting on a ledge of solid stone that this remarkable shrine has been constructed.

64, 65   Beggars

Professional beggars are numerous in all parts of China but it is in the larger cities that they particularly abound. The beggar pursues his calling unmolested, and has even received for himself a recognition and quasi-protection at the hands of the civil authorities. The fact is that the charitable institutions are yet totally unable to cope with the misery and destitution that prevail. No poor-law system is known, and the only plan adopted to palliate the evil is to tolerate begging in public, and to place the *lazaroni* under the local jurisdiction of a responsible chief. In Foochow the city is divided into wards, and within the limits of each ward a headman is appointed who can count his descent from a line of illustrious beggars, and in him rests the right to keep the members of the order under his management and control. During my visit to Foochow I was introduced to one of these beggar kings and he is represented with three of his subjects in the photograph. This king of beggars has it in his power to make an agreement with the shopkeepers of any street which runs through his district, and when a compact of this kind has been concluded, he will protect them from the pestering visits of his gang of beggars.

63

63   The Ma K'uai

This gentleman is known in the city of Foochow as a 'Ma K'uai' (swift as a horse) and holds the position of detective officer attached to the magisterial establishment. He is reported to know the haunts of all the thieves in the district. He has been called the king of thieves and exercises an undoubted sway over the gangs that infest the city.

64

65

66 Foochow

The picture is valuable as it shows the plan of a Chinese house. The street entrance is unfortunately concealed by a wall cutting off the left corner of the foreground. The outer brick wall is raised to the height of the roof and encloses a quadrangular space, the front half being an open court, with apartments to right and left, while to the rear is the dwelling where members of the family reside. The outer doorway is the only access to the walled enclosure. Thus when this is barred, the family is completely secluded from the gaze of the outside world. Indeed it is impossible to see from the street what is going on within the court even when the door is left open, for a wooden screen intervenes. This screen is devised to guard against the importunity and annoyance of the spirits of the dead, which are supposed only to be capable of travelling in straight lines. To obtain the most perfect degree of privacy and seclusion is the primary object in the construction of all Chinese houses of any pretensions.

67   Terraced Hill Near Foochow

III
CHEKIANG AND KIANGSU
NINGPO SHANGHAI AND THE YANGTZE

68   Pagoda Of The Dragon's Glory (*title page*)

This temple is in the neighbourhood of Shanghai on the banks of the Hwang Pu, near the village of Shi Ka Wei. This Pagoda is one of the most ancient structures in the province and the temple, to which it belongs, is a favourite resort during the Ching Ming festival, the time for offering sacrifices to the spirits of deceased ancestors.

69   Fukien Temple, Ningpo

Among the chief attractions of the town of Ningpo is the Tin Hau or 'Queen of Heaven' Temple, the meeting house of the Fukien Guild. It will be noticed that the stone pillars of the central edifice are remarkable for grotesque yet beautiful designs, where the dragon, the national emblem of China, is seen to be the leading figure. This dragon has been cut in high relief round each pillar and made by this means to appear as if sustaining the temple; the same reptile may be discovered carved in low relief on the blocks of stone between the steps, and supporting also the ornament which forms the apex of the roof above.

The dragon wields a potent influence over the people of the Empire. It forms one of the fundamental principles of their system of geomancy and is supposed to exist in every mountain and stream throughout the land. Its control is as firmly believed by the Chinese masses as are the benign effects of the sunshine upon the earth. The dread of disturbing the repose of the dragon spirit as he broods over the soil of China, forms one of the chief obstacles to the opening of mines and to the construction of railroads and telegraphs across the interior of the country.

The Fukien Temple was originally founded during the twelfth century. It was at different times destroyed and rebuilt and was finally raised to its present magnificent proportions about the beginning of the eighteenth century.

69

71   Golden Island

Chinkiang stands at the junction of the Grand Canal with the Yangtsze, a site of great importance. Chin Shan or Golden Island, is a few miles below the city. It is however, an island no longer as the alluvial deposits of the Yangtsze's floods have joined it completely to the right bank of the river. The pagoda-crowned rock presents the boldest and most striking object in the neighbourhood.

72   Puto Island

Puto is one among a group of more than one hundred islands which stud the Chu Shan archipelago, and is under the independent rule of the Abbot of the great Buddhist monastery dedicated to the goddess Kwan Yin. This islet, which is not over four miles long, forms the chief Buddhist centre of the Empire, and is peopled solely by bonzes and nuns, the inmates of some sixty temples scattered among hills and dales there.

The lives of these Buddhist recluses are very low-pitched. They are not engaged, as a rule, in any active works of charity or benevolence, and the highest praise that can be accorded to them is that they refrain from inflicting harm as well as from doing good.

The chief monastery is shown in the photograph. The group of sacred buildings, embowered in rich foliage and backed by the granite-topped hill, the bright colours of the roofs and walls, the sacred lotus lake spanned by a bridge of marble, together make up a picture of rare romantic beauty.

70

70   A Wayside Shrine Near Ningpo

71

72

73   Shanghai Bund 1869

The foreign houses when seen from the river
present a very striking appearance, partaking as
they do of a variety of massive and graceful
designs. The British concession occupies a
space nearly square, facing the stream and
surrounded by creeks. The roads run almost
parallel to the Bund, and have others which
cross them at right angles, and thus the actual
settlement is divided into regular rectangular
blocks.

The roads parallel with the Bund are now
named after the provinces of the Empire, while
the cross streets are called after the chief cities.
The American concession is contained in a strip
of land to the north, approached by a bridge
over the Soochow Creek; while the French are
found on a plot to the south between the British
concession and the Chinese city.

74   The Shanghai Wheelbarrow

It may seem incredible to some of my readers
when I inform them that in Shanghai wheel-
barrows are substituted for cabs! These wheel-
barrows, if they have no other advantages to
recommend them, are at any rate cheap and
comparatively safe. There are a number of
wheelbarrow stands throughout the city, for
these conveyances are in constant demand and
present a striking feature on the Bund when the
hours of business are at an end.

74

75

7

75   Shanghai Bund 1872

Part of the Bund showing a public garden and
the Oriental Bank behind the flagstaff.

76   Shanghai Bund 1872

Buildings on the southern end of the Bund.

77   The Cage

Crimes of the worst order are sometimes punished by starvation in a cage so constructed that the prisoner has the choice of either suspending himself by the neck to relieve his toes, which just touch the board, or of standing on his toes to relieve his neck.

78   The Cangue

The cangue, or collar of wood, is one of the lighter punishments of China, inflicted for minor offences such as petty theft. The nature of the crime as well as the name and residence of the delinquent, if he has any, are inscribed in prominent characters fixed to the cangue. The wearer is usually located in front of the house or shop where the offence was committed, and is forced to depend for food on the charity of passers-by, as the imposing dimensions of the wooden encumbrance prevent him from feeding himself.

The administration of justice in Chinese courts of law is conducted on principles different from those which prevail among western nations. There are no counsel for the prosecution or to defend the accused. Instead of these, certain officers attached to the Yamuns of the Mandarins and in the pay of the presiding judge, make law their special study and are expected to guide him in all technical points. These men however, are not recognised by their government. In addition to these functionaries there are clerks who attend to the business of the courts and draw up the depositions; but there are other persons to be courted by the parties in a suit, who arrange the gifts and bring the case before their superiors.

In a Chinese court, no oaths are administered to the witnesses, and the truth, or some convenient substitute for it, is only disclosed under the dread of punishment, or by actual torture. Should money flow freely from the friends of an offender, truth and justice, it is said, run a fearful risk of being shunted to the wall and crime condoned. Poorer culprits who have no rich allies to aid them, frequently come worse off. In dealing with these offenders, virtue, justice and purity assert themselves in the righteous judge. Penniless pilferers are bambooed, caged, triced up by the thumbs, or suspended by cords; while lying lips are beaten to a pulp, as a suitable lesson to the deceitful and dishonest pauper.

77

78

79 Street Tradesmen, Kiukiang

How many of the total industrial population of China pursue their occupations in the public streets and may truly be described as 'journeymen tradesmen', is a point on which no estimate can be formed. But in every large city they can be counted by the thousand and these accomplished handicraftsmen can be found at every street corner in China—men far too poor ever to aspire to the dignity of a settled shop, seeking their employment in the public highways and by wandering from door to door.

Ahong (extreme left) has spent his days in the streets of Kiukiang. Ahong is a maker of soup and so was his father before him. Born of a 'bouillon'-producing family, he early became a graduate in the mysteries of the small kitchen which he carries about on his rounds, meeting his regular customers at the stated hours, in certain parts of the town.

The gentleman in the centre is a public scribe and is here seen writing a letter at the dictation of a lady. He combines the avocations of a fortune-teller and physician with that of a penman, laying claim as an occulist to special skill, in professing himself able to cure seventy-one disorders of the human eye.

Next in this group we observe the itinerant barber, a man who performs a variety of professional operations on the organs of sense. He is not a surgeon, as was the case of old in Europe, but he must possess a delicate acquaintance with each of the 'gateways of knowledge' situated in the human head.

The two remaining figures on the right represent a wood-turner and his customer, who is examining the make and finish of a wooden ladle.

81 Sawyers At Work

The Chinese contrivance for supporting a block of wood while they cut it up, is a very simple and ingenious one. Like most of the appliances that people have invented, it effectively performs the work for which it was originally designed; but it wears such a primitive look that we might reasonably expect, had we lived in the land 2,000 years ago, we should have found the same type of men doing the same work with the same appliances. This is among the most startling characteristics of China, and one viewed by a foreigner with continual surprise, accustomed as the latter is to western progress, and inspired with an insane desire for novelty. These men of China, at some distant period of the past, must have had people of inventive genius among them who devised their present simple mechanical appliances, each one in its own sphere, adapted to do a certain kind of work in a way which left nothing to be desired by succeeding generations. There is something in all this which might have attractions for Mr. John Ruskin.

82 Reeling Silk

We owe much to China and perhaps a knowledge of the rearing ot the silkworm and the introduction of silk are two of the greatest boons she has conferred upon Western nations. It was one of my most interesting experiences in the country to observe how modest were the aspects of this widespread industry, and how humble, yet sedulous, were the poor labourers whose lowly toil results in robes so magnificent and dearly prized.

In the village where the photograph was taken, all the women as well as the children of sufficient age, were engaged in reeling silk. The machines are of a very primitive make, the most advanced being the one here shown. The labourers will not permit the introduction of anything more complex, and their guilds or trades' unions are so well organised that they can hold their own against employers.

80

80 Spinning Cotton

In China some of the finest mechanical appliances are to be found in a rudimentary form, containing, so to speak, the germs of our own more complex machines. In this cotton spinning machine the left foot is placed upon the beam, which rests in a crescent-shaped axis of iron, so as to keep it in position, while the other extremity of the beam has a pivot which works in an aperture in the wheel. The right foot of the spinner imparts to this beam the eccentric motion which sets the wheel agoing, a belt on the wheel communicating the rotation to three upper spindles. By this contrivance a great velocity is obtained. The spindles not only spin the cotton, but they act as bobbins, and reel the thread as it is spun. Here we have the early dawn of that complex system of mechanism, which now feeds the looms of Bradford and Manchester.

81

82

83   Nanking Arsenal

The Arsenal was built under the auspices of Li Hung-chang. It was the first of its kind in China and stands near the site of the Porcelain Tower outside the south gate of the city. The 'Monastery of Gratitude' as well as the tower were destroyed by the rebels, and the present Arsenal is partly built out of the bricks which had been employed in these structures. The chants of by-gone days that used to issue from the Buddhist courts, filling the air with their dreary mono-tones, are today replaced by less peaceful sounds—by the whirr of engines, the clang of steam-hammers and the reports of guns or rifles which are being tested for use.

In the photograph my readers will recognise a mitrailleuse; on the right of it is a torpedo and rocket tube, a pile of shells, a howitzer, a rocket-stand and a field-gun carriage.

85   Ruins At Tai Ping Kung

Situated about ten miles from Kuikiang it is said
to be the ruins of a Buddhist monastery, one
of the greatest that was ever founded in China.
Judging from the mounds which mark its foundation, this sanctuary must have covered an
extensive area. I found among a number of
interesting blocks of sculpted stones, one or
two representing the back of foreign books as
they appear in the shelves of a library. Possibly
this may point to Ricci's mission to that part of
the province in 1590.

84   Ningpo Ladies

ON THE RIVER YANGTSZE
From Hankow To The Wushan Gorge

The Yangtsze is the greatest river in China and the longest but two in the world. It flows from an unexplored source in the mountains of Tibet for about 3,000 miles and discharges into the China Sea. At present it is known to be navigable for steamers to the Ichang Gorge, a distance of over 1,000 miles above Shanghai.

From the earliest times the watercourses of China have occasioned trouble to the people and perplexity to the rulers. Summer after summer, when the mountain snows have melted in the north, the flooded streams have burst their banks and carried death and destruction over the vast and fertile districts of the plains below; indeed it appears to me that the prevention of disaster, and the security of the Empire in prosperity and peace, have always been dependent upon the exercise of a vigilant and effective supervision over the watercourse throughout the country by the government.

I will now carry the reader with me on a journey to the gorges of the Upper Yangtsze. During the journey I was fortunate to have two American gentlemen for my companions. At Hankow we hired two boats to convey us as far as Ichang. In the smaller of these two craft our Chinese interpreter, the cook and 'the boys' were accommodated; the larger one was for ourselves.

On the 20th January 1871, with flags flying, our expedition quitted Hankow; but we soon lowered our needless colours and settled down to the tedious process of poleing the boats past the native craft which lined the bank in thousands.

When night set in we cast anchor at the foot of Ta Tuen Shan, ten miles above Hankow. Our boat was divided by bulkheads into three compartments: the after one for the accommodation of the skipper Wang and his wife; the next formed our sleeping bunk; and the forward one furnished with a stove, was converted into a sort of sitting-room. We passed an intensely cold night for the wind blew through every crevice into the cabin, and we were forced next morning to make a liberal application of paper and paste to prevent a repetition of the inconvenience.

As we advanced we were favoured with a slight wind, the sails were then spread, and the men squatted about the deck to enjoy their

86   Homes Of Foreign Settlers, Hankow

pipes and the cheering prospect of a fair breeze and no work to be done. The Yangtsze was now about a mile broad and its waters were of a dark chocolate hue. The banks were low, furrowed or terraced with high-water marks left by the floods. These clay walls have a dark and tragic history, if one could but decipher it. Fragments of projecting wood here and there crop out from the clay—the broken remnants of some homestead, deposited with the debris of a long-forgotten flood. It is slow travelling in these Chinese boats; the old stagecoach had the speed of lightning in comparison with them. During the early part of the voyage we suffered greatly from cold, as the coal we had with us would not burn.

The wind died away at sunset and we anchored for the night at Pai Tsu, forty-six miles above Hankow. Next morning we were up early but could effect no start till seven o'clock; for Wang was in his bed aft, and his crew were forward, stowed snugly in the hold. An interesting dialogue thereore ensued. The skipper pointed out to his men the propriety of their turning to; and they in reply, insisted that it was the captain's duty to be himself the first at his post. On this our second day in West Reach we passed a long sand-pit not shown on the Admiralty chart, and next morning we sighted the Pan Thi rock, which rises in mid-stream about a quarter of a mile distant from the left bank. At this place the river was about two miles wide, and at the end of the reach is the entrance to the lake stream, which debouches from the mouth of the Tung Ting Lake. Very beautiful scenery is to be found in this district of the Yangtsze. The banks at the season of our visit presented a bold and striking front to the vast expanse of water, while in the vapoury distance we could descry a line of white sails, those of a fleet of trading junks, as if pictured in the clouds, travelling far away into space. Beyond the Tung Ting Lake the Yangtsze is known simply as the Ta Kiang or Great River.

87

We had a day of snow, and there being no wind the men were compelled to track the boat up stream with a bamboo line affixed to the mast. After this, for some days, the routine of sailing and tracking was only equalled in mono- tony by the sameness of the scenery around. There was an endless flow of still and silent water, and the level plains on either bank, with- out a single object of interest to break the even line. At length, on the 27th, we landed at a pretty, rustic hamlet, beautiful in its quiet repose, and where everything seemed to have gone to rest for the winter. This village stretched along the crest of an embankment, and was backed by skeleton trees whose snow-clad branches stood out coldly against a leaden sky. The red light of reed fires gleamed from the open doorways and sparkled in the oyster-shell windows. There was no one astir, not a footprint had marred the icy mantle in which the soil was wrapped.

Our interpreter Chang was, I regret to say, of little service; for no member of our party understood his dialect thoroughly, and I found my own Hainan men, who spoke the Kwang- tung dialect and Malay fluently, of much greater use. Chang however, had influence with the boatmen, who looked up to him on account of his literary attainment. He was useful as a master of ceremonies in the presence of officials, and he also kept a careful journal. There he is, presented to the reader in No 88, just after he had been droning, in an obscure corner of the cabin, over a whole classical commentary. The figure to the left is one of the boatmen, while a Ningpo boy is looking from the cabin door.

We next halted at Shang Chai Wan, a small town, where we were able to purchase some excellent coal.

On Feb 2nd we reached the great trading mart Shansi, about three hundred miles above Hankow. Here the river is one and a-half miles broad, and the town is situated on the left bank of one of the finest reaches of the Yangtsze.

We are now entering the mountain region of

the Upper Yangtsze, and could see in the distance the dim outline of mountains which rise about 3,000 feet above the bed of the stream. The river at this point is from four to five miles broad, its bottom is hard and pebbly and dangerous shoals abound.

Feb 4th. Passed a rocky point, where men were fishing with otters. These animals, which appeared quite tame and tractable, were attached to the boats by long cords. They dived readily if gently pushed by their proprietors, and coming up when they had made a capture, freely yielded their prey to the fishermen. The towns and villages which bordered the river in this portion of the provinces of Hupeh and Hunan wore an air of solid prosperity, which contrasted favourably with the regions below. The same was observable in the well-tilled soil and in the general aspect of the people.

Feb 5th brought us in sight of Ichang Pagoda. Here the hills on the right bank fall in a series of bold cliffs into the river, and above rise the mountains in a chaos of cloud-piercing peaks and crags. At Ichang we witnessed a naval review. About a dozen boats, such as that shown in No. 89 made up the Imperial fleet, and I was much impressed with the strangeness of the scene, for behind these puny war boats the deep blue ranges of Ichang upreared their lofty masses and shut us in all round in an amphitheatre of hills. The boats were moored in double line, and each was gay with flags and streamers of brilliant and beautiful hues. Their artillery practice was however, defective, the firing being very irregular, some of the guns unwilling to be discharged at all. We visited one of these fighting craft, and among other things which we found on board were rifle-stands supporting wooden rifles placed, as it would seem, in conspicuous places to strike terror into the heart of the enemy.

We left our Hankow boats at Ichang to await our return from the gorges, and hired a suitable rapids boat to carry us to Kweichow in Szechuan.

91

92

93

94

Our new crew consisted of twenty-four wiry fellows, men accustomed to the dangers of the gorges, and to the poor fare and hard work to be encountered there.

We left this inland port on the 7th Feb and in a few hours had entered the mouth of Ichang Gorge, fourteen miles above the city. The mountains here vary in height from 500 to 2,500 feet, and the Great River flows through a narrow cleft, in some places not more than a hundred yards across. The channel is every-where deep and clear, gloomily overshadowed by the rocky walls which frown in gigantic precipices on both sides of the stream. Rude fisher-huts, perched here and there upon the lofty cliffs, afford the only evidence of the presence of man. It is in such desolate spots as these that the frugality and industry of the Chinese race are most conspicuously exhibited. A number of the hardy natives live by fishing, while others are engaged in the stone quarries close by; and wherever it is at all possible, the thin soil on the face of the rocks is scraped and planted with vegetables.

The next day was the first night of the Chinese New Year, and the boatmen spent the afternoon at a village on the right bank of the river. A number of our crew proceeded to a temple to make sacrifice, and later in the evening I was called upon to adjust a dispute. Chang protested that his honourable name had been sullied by the drunken behaviour of the boat-men. I however, discovered quickly that our venerated interpreter was himself not without sin being, indeed, unable to stand erect. The crew spent the night in drinking, gambling and opium-smoking, rioting noisily and firing crack-ers from time to time. In the morning the skipper sacrificed a cock to the river goddess and cast some wine upon the waters.

Two or three miles above the village we encountered the first rapid, and here we en-gaged additional hands to tow us up the stream. This task they accomplished by fixing a strong bamboo tugline to the masthead, while a second rope was made fast to a rock at the top of the rapid, and hauled in on deck so that we might be kept in position if the towing line gave way. The trackers, fifty in number, each with his bamboo loop slung over the shoulders and attached to the towing-line, were crawling forward inch by inch, hands and feet firmly planted in the rocks on the bank, till at length they launched the labouring boat into the smooth waters above. The Lukan Gorge, which we entered on the afternoon of the 9th, pre-sented a scene yet grander than any which we had hitherto encountered. Here the mountains are more than 3,000 feet high, and sheer precipices of 1,000 feet rose up from the very margin of the water. Photograph No. 95

Next morning, we ascended the great rapid of Tsing Tan, at the mouth of Mi Tan Gorge. This rapid is one of the grandest spectacles in the whole panorama of the Upper Yangtsze. The river presents a smooth surface as it emerges from the pass. Suddenly it seems to bend like a polished cylinder of glass, falls eight or ten feet, and then, curving upwards in a glorious crest of foam, it surges away in wild tumult down the river.

We made fast for the night at the small town of Kwei in Hupeh. This is built on sloping ground beneath the cliffs on the left bank of the river. It was puzzling to imagine on what the people can subsist. There were no cultivated lands, no boats, nor signs of any sort of trade; the only being we encountered was a solitary beggar, and he was anxious to depart from Kwei. There are a number of coal mines near Patung which provides work for the villagers.

Wushan Gorge, which we entered on the morning of the 13th, is more than twenty miles in length and the river here was perfectly placid, the mountains rising in confused masses to a great altitude. We reached Wushan in Szechuan and terminated our journey at this point, a dis-tance of over 1,200 miles from Shanghai.

97   Wushan Tower, Szechuan

Wushan Tower, one of the most remarkable structures in this part of the Upper Yangtsze, was built originally in the early half of the sixth century, when the Ch'in dynasty was on the throne, and the site then selected was the house of a wineseller named Hsing. The tower was demolished by the Taipings and barely three years have elapsed since it was completely restored. It now rests on a platform of solid masonry, rising boldly from the bank of the river, and the sole relic of the original structure is an ancient monument to be seen in front of the tower, upon which, if we are to believe the legend, the saintly founder alighted from the sky to partake there of a spiritual repast and wake the echoes with a melody on his flute. It was the year 202 B.C. or thereabouts, that this incident occurred, and we are told that the sage, whose name was Fli Wei, managed his aerial flight on the back of a stork. Storks may still be found, but there are no musical sages to use them now.

It was not without difficulty that I obtained a picture of this tower. I found the court in front of the edifice filled with the customary crowd of idlers who loiter in the precincts of the temples: beggars, fortune-tellers, hawkers, city roughs and street boys. I was therefore compelled to retire within the city wall in order to avoid the throng. The gate was then shut to, but still the mob managed to scale the ramparts, perfectly civil indeed, but intensely curious to watch my operations, some doubtless imagining that I intended to open fire on the town, as they saw my camera pointed through the ramparts. The weather was against me as well, for a high wind charged with clouds of sand was blowing upstream, and stirring up so great a tempest that the only boats to be seen as we crossed the river were the well-equipped craft which bore 'The Great Peace Save Life Boats' inscribed in huge black characters on their sides.

96

97

IV
NORTH CHINA
PEKING

金俱房一影橋

119

98   The Drum Tower (*title page*)

99   The Central Street In The Chinese Quarter Of Peking

Peking consists of two cities: one the Tartar or Manchu city with the Imperial Palace in its centre and the other the Chinese, containing the Altars of Heaven and Earth where the State worship is carried on.

The Tartar city is enclosed by massive walls, nearly in the form of a square, each side measuring about three and a-half miles. These walls are pierced with nine gates; three on the south side and two on each of the others.

The Tartar city is supposed to contain nothing except the Imperial Palace, the abodes of the nobles and the barracks for the accommodation of the bannermen who form the bodyguard of the Emperor. Several causes however, have contributed to alter this the original state of things; the most prominent of which are the long residence of these bannermen in the capital, their familiar intercourse with the less warlike Chinese, their proud disdain for trades or handicrafts of every sort and the inadequate support which the government allowances can supply. Many of the old families of the Manchu bannermen have thus become impoverished and the lands allotted to them at the time of the conquest have been sold and have passed to Chinese proprietors; so that now there is a considerable Chinese population to be found within the Tartar city.

The Chinese city adjoins the southern wall of the Tartar city. It is also walled in the form of a parallelogram and covers an area five miles long by three broad. Access to this division of the metropolis is gained through seven gateways—two on the north, one eastward, one westward and three others on the southern side.

This photograph is taken from the city wall of Peking close to the Ch'ienmen or central gate, between the Chinese and Tartar quarters. It is in direct line with the centre·of the Palace and is the route which the Emperor traverses on his way to the Altar of Heaven. In the foreground we see a white marble bridge which spans a kind of city moat. This street, like all the thoroughfares in the Tartar city, is a very wide one and is a place of great concourse and traffic.

100   Chinese Ministers Of State

Shên Kwei Fên (left) President of the Board of War and Member of the Grand Council, is fifty-six years of age.
Tung Hsün (centre) President of the Board of Finance, a celebrated scholar and author of historical and topographical works. He is sixty-one years of age.
Mao Ch'ang Hsi, President of the Board of Works, is fifty-six years of age.

The Government of China may be divided into central, provincial and extra-provincial. The first division comprises the holders of high office in Peking; the second the governors of the eighteen provinces of China proper and the three provinces of Manchuria. In the third class we may place the officials resident in those vast regions known as Inner and Outer Mongolia, Sinkiang and Tibet.

Every Manchu mandarin of high standing has military as well as civil rank. The Manchu army, which conquered China in 1644, was divided originally into four corps distinguished by the white, red, blue and yellow banners under which they fought. Four bordered banners of the same colours were subsequently added and in the course of time, eight corps of Mongols and eight of Chinese who had sided with the invader were established.

The chief commands of these are shared among high officers of the three races, the Manchu on the whole being the predominating class. Prince Kung is General of one banner, Wên Hsiang of another, Pao Chün and Ching Lien of the third and fourth. Each of these officials is also the head of some principal department in the central administration. The Grand Secretariat is made up of four chief and two assistant secretaries, these posts being shared in equal proportion between Chinese, Mongols and Manchus. Next in degree to this office are six Boards representing departments in the administration. These are the Board of Civil Service, the Board of Finance, the Board of Rites, Obligations and Observances, the Board of War, the Board of Criminal Jurisdiction and the Board of Public Works. Each of these boards has two chief officers or Presidents, one a Manchu and the other a Chinese.

The real power of the Central Government may be said to reside in the Great Council

which was established shortly after the foundation of the Manchu dynasty, its members appointed not on the recommendation of the departments, but by the Emperor's own choice. At the moment it has five members, Prince Kung, Wên Hsiang, Pao Chün, Shên Kuei Fên and the Emperor's private tutor.

These Ministers are also members of the Tsungli Yamen established in 1861 to deal with foreign affairs. Prince Kung presides over this Council and its members are ministers of the highest rank in the Empire, including the Manchus, Wên Hsiang, Pao Chün, and Ching Lien, and the Chinese, Shên Kuei Fên, Tung Hsün and Mao Ch'ang Hsi.

In the provinces Governors are at the head of affairs—in some cases a Governor-General or Viceroy may have more than one province under his rule, thus Jui Lin is Governor-General of Kwangtung and Kwangsi. Governors have each a small body of troops at their disposal but they do not command the naval or military forces of the provinces. Generally in provincial capitals permanent Manchu garrisons under Manchu officers are established whereas the Chinese forces are under a separate officer and a series of subordinates, but whose troops exist principally on paper.

The civil functionaries play a part that is much more real. A province is divided into a number of districts and officered by magistrates and assistant magistrates. A group of districts forms a department and this is ruled by a prefect or sub-prefect. A number of these departments again makes up a circuit, of which there may be several in a province. Add to this a commissioner of finance, one of criminal justice, one of the commissariat and one of the salt revenue and you have, without pretension to minute accuracy, a fair resumé of the machinery by which the Government of China is supposed to be carried on.

101   Prince Kung

Prince Kung, now about forty years of age, is the sixth son of the Emperor Tao-kuang who reigned from 1820–1850. He is the younger brother of the late Emperor Hsien-feng and consequently an uncle to the reigning Emperor T'ung-chih. Prior to 1860 he was little known beyond the precincts of the Court; but when the Emperor fled from the Summer Palace, it was he who came forward to meet the Ministers of the Allied Powers and negotiate the conditions of peace. He holds several high civil and military appointments, the most important that of member of the Supreme Council. Quick of apprehension, open to advice and comparatively liberal in his views, he is the acknowledged leader of that small group of Chinese politicians comprising the party of progress.

Independently of his various offices Prince Kung as his title denotes, is a member of the highest order of Chinese nobility, an expression which to prevent misconception, we must beg our readers' permission to explain. There have been from the most ancient times in China, five degrees of honour to which men whose services have been eminent may attain. Their male heirs however, cannot succeed to the title without revival of their patent and even then, as a rule, the title they succeed to is one degree less honourable than that of their predecessor; so that were the usage in vogue with us, a dukedom would dwindle to a baronetcy in five generations.

The Manchu family which rules the country, or to speak more correctly those of the stock who are within a certain degree of the Imperial line, have no less than eighteen orders of nobility, liable however, like the old system spoken of above, to gradual extinction except in a few particular instances where the patent ensures the title of perpetuity. Prince Kung received such a patent in 1865.

102

103

102–105   Ministers Of State

Wên Hsiang, a Manchu Minister of State, born in Mukden in 1817. He ranks next to Prince Kung on the Board of Foreign Affairs and has held the position since 1861. He is also a Member of the Grand Council, President of the Board of Civil Service and Member of the Imperial Cabinet. His rare intellectual powers, coupled with his long experience in high office, cause Wên Hsiang to be looked upon as the most influential statesman in China.

Pao Chün, a Manchu and Member of the Grand Council, is one of the Presidents of the Board of Finance. He is now sixty-five years of age.

Ching Lien is the youngest Member of the Board of Foreign Affairs, being not yet more than forty-five.

Li Hung-chang, born in 1823, is at present Viceroy of Peichihli, and stands foremost among the Viceroys of the eighteen provinces of China. He is the first Han Chinese to be so honoured.

104   105

106   The Hall Of Classics

West of the Yung-lo Kung, the great lamasery, where a living Buddha rules, stands the college attached to the Confucian Temple and known as the Kwo Tze Kung. In this building, prior to the reign of Ch'ien-lung, the ancient Classics were expounded. But that Emperor determined to imitate a much more ancient structure and accordingly built the edifice known as the Pi Yung Kung, or the Hall of Classics, which is seen here through the archway. The building is square. Its upper roof rests on a series of carved wooden brackets; pillars of wood also support the lower one and the whole is crowned with a gilded copper ball. The base is marble, and the edifice is approached by four bridges of the same material spanning a marble-walled moat, surrounded with white marble balustrades.

The Hall stands in the centre of a court, and on the right and left of it, in long open verandahs, there are about two hundred tablets of upright stone. On these tablets the complete text of the nine Classics has been engraved, an idea repeated from the Han and Tang dynasties. In front there is a yellow porcelain triple archway or pai-lau, having the inner portion of its arches built of white marble.

107   Lee Shen-lan And His Pupils

Lee Shen-lan is Professor of Mathmatics in the
Imperial College, Peking, and is now about
sixty years of age. He is pictured here surrounded by his pupils.

108   Peking Observatory

Near to the Palace and on the east side of the
Tartar city the Observatory is to be seen. This
Observatory was erected during the Yuen or
Mongol dynasty, towards the end of the thir-
teenth century. The instruments shown here
were constructed under the superintendence of
Father Verbiest in the seventeenth century. The
globe itself is brazen, exactly round and smooth;
the stars well made and in their true places.
It is so well hung that the least touch moves it,
though it is above 2,000 lbs in weight. The
armillary sphere consists of circles which are
divided into 360 degrees and each degree into
sixty minutes, as in Europe.

The stars on this celestial globe are all
raised brass and distinguished according to
their magnitude, for the convenience of feeling
on a dark night.

107

108

109

109   The Bell Tower

The Bell Tower is situated about a quarter of a
mile beyond the North Gate and contains one
of the five great bells cast in the reign of Yung-
lo. Each of these bells weighs about fifty-three
tons. All but one are perfect examples of the
art of casting metal, as are the astronomical
instruments belonging to the same period. The
Tower bell has a rich mellow tone, which can
easily be distinguished, when the watches are
struck at midnight, all over Peking.

110   Bronze Temple, Wan Shou Shan

This is one of the most interesting buildings in
the grounds of the Imperial Summer Palace,
standing at the foot of Wan Shou Shan, upon
a base of white marble and constructed—doors,
windows, pillars, roofs and all—entirely of
solid bronze. It is a very perfect example of
Chinese temple architecture showing the most
minute details of construction and the skill
with which the Chinese can work in metals and
adapt them to almost every use.

112 Cenotaph Erected To The Panjim Lama Of Tibet

This monument stands more than a mile beyond the north wall of the city, in the huge pile of buildings known as the Hwang-she.

The Panjim is second only to the Dalai Lama and is also looked upon as a lesser incarnation of Buddha. As Tibet owes an allegiance to China, the Emperor conceived a jealousy of the friendly reception extended to the English by the Panjim and therefore courteously invited his holiness to visit Peking. Sensing treachery, he nevertheless set out from Lhasa on the 15th of July, 1779 and reached Peking early in the following year. His worst fears were realised. After being feted as a divinity and worshipped in person by the Emperor, he was in due time attacked by smallpox (so the story goes) and died in the chamber adjoining his reception hall. It has been strongly suspected that he was poisoned at the Emperor's suggestion.

The remarkable monument seen in the picture was erected at immense cost to commemorate the Lama's visit and is built of white marble after the Tibetan model. The bell-like cupola and the upper ornaments are of gold, and the whole is most elaborately carved with allegorical subjects.

111 Koreans

Korea is one of the nations tributary to China and although her King may be esteemed an independent sovereign, he yet sends an annual embassy of tribute-bearers to Peking. I happened to be in the capital in 1871 when that embassy arrived and I was fortunate in obtaining this picture of two of the officers.

113 A Pekingese Pai-Lau

This Pai-lau or Chinese honorary portal, is erected at the gate of the Ta Ka Tien Temple which the Emperor visits when he prays for rain. Structures of this sort are very numerous in Peking. A man may obtain permission to erect a pai-lau in honour of himself or children; many erect one in honour of deceased parents. In ancient times, these triple gates were to be met with crossing the trade routes of the interior, when they were inscribed with directions for the traveller regarding the route to be followed and the distance to different towns.

111

114   A Peking Home

The dwelling is that of Mr. Yang, a gentleman enormously rich and holding an official rank in Peking. His abode, like all others of its kind, is walled around and can be entered only by a plain doorway through a high brick wall which skirts an obscure alley. Within the door were two silk lanterns, dangling from supports above and daubed with the name and titles of Yang. An inner court opened into a sort of paradise with a miniature lotus lake spanned by a marble bridge.

In the photograph are Mr. Yang, his son and a party of ladies, younger children and maids of the household.

115   A Small Courtyard In Mr. Yang's House
116   Interior Of The Reception Hall
(*page 136*)

117,118   Manchu Ladies (*page 137*)

The Manchu or Tartar lady may, on the whole, be said to approach more nearly than her Chinese sister to our western notions of female beauty and grace. The former enjoys greater freedom and her feet which are never compressed, appear to be naturally small and well formed. Their rich dresses too, are always elegant. The full robes of a lady and gentleman of the wealthier classes are highly picturesque and remarkable also for the richness and beauty of their materials. The costume is ample, graceful and well adapted to the climate, light in summer and warm enough in winter.

115

116

117

118

119–122   Female Coiffure

Represented here is the coiffure of married
Manchu matrons, which differs widely from
anything Chinese. Nos. 120 and 121 show
respectively the full front and full back views.
The basis of this coiffure consists of a flat strip
of wood, ivory or precious metal about a foot
in length. Half of the real hair of the wearer is
gathered up and twisted in broad bands around
this support, which is then laid across the back
of the head. The style is simple and graceful
and must have been designed, one would almost
think, to represent horns, enabling the wearer to
hold her own against her antagonistic husband.

119

120

121

122

124   A Peking Shop

The shops of Peking differ in many respects from those in the cities of Southern China. The former are closed in front with ornamental partitions of hard wood, having narrow arched doorways. Above these doorways are blinds, or sunshades which can be raised and spread out horizontally in front of the shops. The balustrade above presents always some Chinese design, very pretty, both in its open latticework and in the huge characters which denote the name and occupation of the tradesman. We gather, from the large gilt characters above, that cotton and Manchester goods are imported and, from the signboards below, that silk, satin and other fabrics may also be bought here; while the pedestal in front supports the announcement that the great foot measure is alone used in this establishment.

123   A Travelling Fruitseller

This man carries his shop on his shoulders and we see him here informing the dwellers in a narrow lane that he has brought to their doors the choicest grapes of the season.

124

125

125, 126   Manchu Soldiers

On Sept 18, 1871, I witnessed a review of an
army of men such as these, on the plain which
stretches northwards outside the Anting gate of
the Tartar city. Many of the troops assembled
there were armed with bows and arrows and
many more with old fuse matchlocks shown in
No. 125, while in the belt a row of breech-
loading cartridges were stored.

126

127

127   A Travelling Chiropodist

This travelling chiropodist is operating on a corn
and dressing the toenails of a customer; while
a second patient waits placidly until his own
turn arrives, smoking the pipe of peace from a
broken window.

128   Travelling Antique Dealers

129   Funeral Bannermen

The Manchu funeral procession is elaborate and
costly, the coffin may be borne by sixty-four
men and perhaps the canopy which covers it is
of richly embroidered white satin. The hired
bannermen who take part in the procession are
shown in the photograph. They are commonly
beggars dressed up by the undertaker for the
purpose.

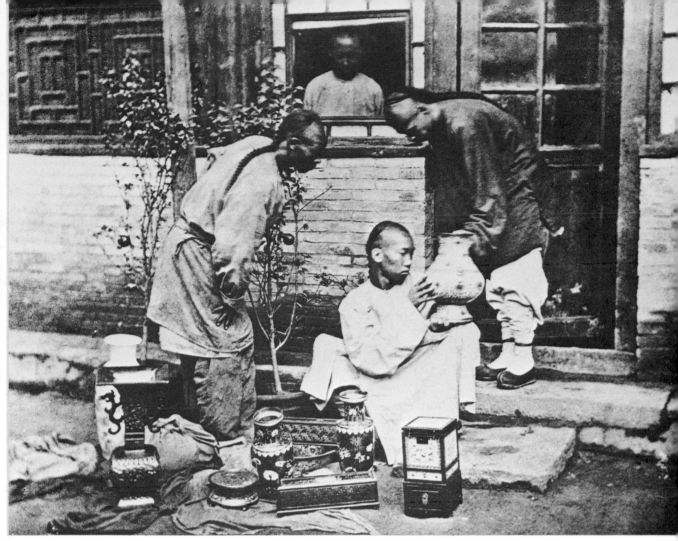

128

129

130   Scrap Collector

Such men as our old friend here, are employed to collect scraps of printed paper which are afterwards burned before some shrine. This is however, only one branch of his business—he picks up rags and bones from the dust-heaps as well and disposes of his miscellaneous collection to some dealer when the day's work is done. Poor and miserable as he seems, he is not without a family and friends of his own, and his old age gains him respect.

130

131   One Of The City Guard, Peking

The subject of this picture is an old Tartar bannerman who kept watch at the gate of a hotel by night. Wrapped in his sheepskin coat and in an underclothing of rags, he lay through the cold nights on the stone steps of the outer gateway and only roused himself at times to answer the call of his fellow watchmen near at hand. This call is supposed to be passed from watchman to watchman all round the city. Wang, as he is called, employed also a wooden clapper to let the inmates know he was astir, and to scare away thieves.

131

The Imperial pleasure-grounds lie about eight miles to the north-west of Peking and the Yuan Ming Yuan is the name by which they are most commonly known. Wan Shou Shan, a hill within its surroundings is the portion best known to foreigners. This summer retreat, with its palaces, lakes and gardens, covers an area of twelve square miles and was laid out by the Emperor K'ang-hsi. It must at one time have been a fascinating spot, and even as I saw it, in its ruins, and as the Allied forces had laid it waste and left it, there was a charm about it all its own. The whole presents us with a Chinese landscape garden. White marble bridges span lakes bedecked with lotus flowers, where summer pavilions rise among the inlets on every side. The hills too, are crowned with temples and pagodas and herds of deer and other sorts of game wander in the woods that shade many a ruined palace.

The marble bridge in the picture contains seventeen arches and is the finest that I have seen in China or indeed in the East.

The hill descried in the distance is Wan Shou Shan and is surmounted by a temple built of white marble and porcelain. This temple, like the bridge, has been left almost uninjured, although two lions of white marble and colossal in size, which stand at the base of the stonework, have been destroyed by fire.

Nothing has been attempted in the way of restoration. Indeed I suppose that the Chinese have neither the spirit nor the funds to enter upon such an arduous undertaking, or that the place is left ruinous and desolate as an ever-ready witness to the wanton barbarities to which foreigners will resort. Many of the educated Chinese have this feeling and look upon our conduct as an act of heartless vandalism, and say that we might have brought pressure to bear upon their government in some way more worthy of our much vaunted civilisation.

133   The Great Sacrificial Hall At The Tomb Of The Emperor Yung-lo

Before the Sacrificial Hall is reached the visitor has to pass through an outer hall and a marble paved court into the second or sacrificial quadrangle where Imperial offerings are still made to the Emperor of a former dynasty. This photograph was taken from the marble platform of the outer hall and gives a front view of the court and Hall of Sacrifice.

The Hall has a splendid interior and the thirty-two teak pillars from Yunan, which support the lower roof, must have been kings of the forest. Each of these pillars is four feet in span and thirty-two feet in height. The outer roof of this building is covered with yellow glazed tiles and the eaves project ten feet outside the walls.

Beyond the main edifice there is still another court and to the north of that, a well-built tunnel, thirty yards long, conducts through the burial ground to the doorway of the tomb.

Three miles to the south of the Imperial Palace in the Chinese quarter of Peking, is an extensive park-like enclosure, containing the Temple and the Open Altar of Heaven. Both are built of marble and both have triple terraces surrounded by marble balustrading. One supports in its centre a building of triple roofs, covered with light blue tiles and symbolical of heaven; while the other has a plain round marble platform on top, open to heaven, where the Emperor offers sacrifice to Shan-ti, the Supreme Lord of Heaven and Earth, at the winter solstice on the 21st December. Such altars as these seem to be relics of an extremely ancient and primitive form of worship in China, before the advent of Confucius and the Buddhist faith.

135

137 The Pekingese Mule Litter

This is the usual conveyance adopted by the Chinese, if they wish for ease and comfort, when they visit localities outside the Great Wall. Two long shafts support the litter and are harnessed at the ends to the backs of two mules. It was to this chair that I consigned myself on the occasion of my journey to the Great Wall.

138 The Pekingese Camel

At certain seasons of the year, camels may be encountered in tens of thousands crossing the desert of Gobi, laden with brick tea, on their way to the Russian frontier. This brick tea, in the absence of metallic currency, forms the circulating medium in Mongolia, Siberia and Tibet. When in the province of Peichihli, I witnessed the departure of a train of 2,000 of these camels laden with brick tea to be sold in the Russian markets.

136 Stone Animals, Ming Tombs

The tombs of the Ming Emperors of China stand about thirty miles north of Peking and in their general design resemble those of Nanking. They are however, in their dimensions still more imposing than even the tomb of Hung-wu, the first sovereign of the dynasty.

In this valley of tombs, which is backed by a crescent-shaped range of hills having a radius of from two to three miles, the mausolea of thirteen Ming sovereigns are to be found. The first interred there was Ch'eng Tsu (better known as Yung-lo), the third monarch of the dynasty.

The tomb of Yung-lo is approached first through an avenue of animals, sculpted out of white limestone, and then through a double row of stone warriors. All the figures wear an expression of tranquil repose, thoroughly in keeping with their duty as guardians of the dead. As to the animals, there are two pairs of each kind, two kneeling and two standing upright. Thus we first meet two pairs of lions, then two pairs of unicorns; these are followed by two pairs of camels, one of which is shown in the foreground. Two pairs of elephants succeed, and beyond these are two pairs of fabulous animals called 'kylin', and still further on are the mail-clad warriors.

136

139   Nankow Pass

We enter the Nankow Pass about thirty miles
distance from Peking. This pass is a bold, rocky
defile, separating China proper from the land
of the barbarians beyond.

154

140 Ancient Buddhist Arch At Kew
     Yung Kwan, Nankow Pass

In the village of Kew Yung Kwan in the Nankow
Pass, there is a very remarkable marble arch
erected during the Yuan dynasty. The arch is
octagonal in form and adorned with strange
figures from Indian mythology. The keystone
carries a mythological figure flanked with two
others wearing crowns of a seven-headed snake,
while the bodies of the snakes flow into the
ornamentation on either side. The interior of the
arch is also elaborately sculptured. The upper
surfaces are covered with a multitude of small
images of Buddha carved in bas-relief. An old
inscription on the inner surface dates the erection of the arch to about A.D. 1345.

141　The Great Wall Of China

My readers doubtless share with me in feeling that no illustrated work on China would be worthy of its name if it did not contain a picture of the Great Wall. This wall is an object neither picturesque nor striking. Viewing it simply as a wall we find its masonry often defective, and it is not so solid or honestly constructed as one at first sight would imagine. It is only in the best parts that it has been faced with stone or rather, that it consists of two retaining walls of stone and a mound of earth within.

The wall was built to save the country from the raids of the nomadic northern hordes and this object it actually attained; thus Genghis Khan himself was repulsed before the inner wall.

The erection of the Great Wall, which has a length of 1500 miles, was the last great work of the Emperor Tsin She-hwang, 213 B.C. (Ch'in Dynasty). This view was taken from the north of the inner wall, at a place called Pata Ling.

The inner wall stretches across the northern end of the Nankow Pass and climbs in many places to almost inaccessible steeps. It was built originally about A.D. 542 and is about 500 miles in length, its extremities joining on to the older outer wall. It is furnished with square watchtowers at short distances apart in the passes and at longer distances in less accessible regions. The height of the wall is over thirty feet and it is about fourteen feet broad on the top.

To venture upon any further description of this ancient barrier would only be to repeat an oft-told story with which my reader is perhaps, already well acquainted. I will conclude therefore, by expressing the hope that the work will convey a faithful impression of the places over which my journey extended and of the people as I found them, so that my five years' labour may not have been in vain.

TECHNIQUE

THE WET COLLODION PROCESS

The Negative
Only glass plates free from scratches, bubbles and blemishes to be used. Place glass in a plate holder (a wooden frame with a screw vice) and clean by rubbing the glass with a mixture of Tripoli powder and alcohol. The plate is dried with filtering or Japanese paper. (The plate must not be touched by the fingers.)

Preparation of Collodion
Collodion is a thick transparent liquid which solidifies when exposed to the air. It is made by dissolving gun-cotton in a mixture of alcohol and ether. A viscous syrupy liquid is obtained after 48 hours and this can be kept until it is required to be sensitized.

Coating the Plate with Collodion
This is done in the dark room (or tent). The plate is held by one corner and a small quantity of collodion is poured on to the middle of the plate. which is inclined so that the liquid covers the entire surface. The liquid must not be allowed to flow twice over the same spot as this would produce an uneven level and it must be free of streaks, bubbles, etc.

Sensitizing the Plate
The collodion is allowed a few seconds to set and it is then immersed in the sensitizing silver bath. This light sensitive solution is nitrate of silver to which certain other chemicals have been added. The whole surface of the collodion must be brought into contact with the silver bath at the same moment. A dish containing the liquid is tilted and one edge of the plate placed at the high end. The plate is then lowered into the liquid by means of a silver hook.

Development of Image
After the plate has been exposed in the camera, it is removed from the dark slide in the darkroom (or tent). A solution of protosulphate of iron, distilled water, acetic acid and alcohol made just before it is required, is the developing liquid which is poured rapidly and repeatedly over the surface of the plate until the image is developed. When the exposure is well-timed the picture appears gradually "as if by enchantment, clear, pure, sharp; the details are admirably distinct, the lights are free from stains and the blacks are represented by distinct tones varying according to the depths of the shadows."

Fixing the Negative

It is necessary to remove all the iodide of silver which has not been affected by the exposure as this would darken the negative when again exposed to the light. Hyposulphite of soda is used for this purpose (also cyanide of potassium). After all the unaltered iodide of silver has been removed the plate is washed in water.

The negative is now finished but a coat of varnish or gum arabic may be applied to protect the surface.

Adapted from *'A History and Handbook of Photography'* by Gaston Tissandier, edited by John Thomson and published in 1876.

BIBLIOGRAPHY

Books written and illustrated by John Thomson

The Antiquities of Cambodia   A series of twelve photographs with descriptions (Edinburgh 1867)
Views on the North River   Description of places in Kwangtung, China, with fourteen photographs (Hong Kong 1870)
Illustrations of China and Its People   A series of two hundred photographs with descriptions of the places and people represented. Published in four volumes (London 1873)
The Land and the People of China   A cheap version of *Illustrations of China and Its People,* with engravings made from Thomson's photographs. (New York 1876)
The Straits of Malacca, Indo-China and China, or Ten Years Travels, Adventures and Residence Abroad. Illustrated with engravings made from Thomson's photographs. (London 1876)
Street Life of London   Twelve monthly instalments with three photographs in each instalment (London 1877)
Through Cyprus with the Camera in the Autumn of 1878–79   Descriptions of places and people with sixty photographs. Published in two volumes (London 1879)
Through China with a Camera (London 1898)

ACKNOWLEDGMENTS

The photograph of John Thomson which appears on page eight is from the John Hillelson—B.S. Kahn Collection, London. It is reproduced by permission of John Hillelson.

The photographs numbered 22, 38, 93 and 94 are among those donated to the Royal Geographical Society, London, by John Thomson. They are reproduced here for the first time by permission of the Royal Geographical Society.